Piano • Vocal • Guitar

W9-CWE-269

TOP COUNTRY HITS
2010 - 2011

ISBN 978-1-61780-719-0

HAL•LEONARD®
CORPORATION
7777 W. BLUEMOUND RD. P.O. BOX 13819 MILWAUKEE, WI 53213

Visit Hal Leonard Online at
www.halleonard.com

ALL ABOUT TONIGHT

Words and Music by RHETT AKINS,
DALLAS DAVIDSON and BEN HAYSLIP

Don't both-er tell-in' me what
Hey, pret-ty thing, ___ I've been

I got com-in' in the morn-in'. I al-read-y know. ___
look-in' at you since the mo-ment that you walked ___ in. ___

I got some feel-good pills ___ and a red ___
I've got some wild-ass bud-dies that love ___

mor - row can wait __ till to - mor - row. It's all a - bout to - night.

night.

It's all a - bout to -

6

BACK TO DECEMBER

Words and Music by
TAYLOR SWIFT

These days I have-n't been sleep-in'; stay-in' up, play-in' back my - self leav - in',

when your birth - day passed ___ and I did - n't call. ___

D.S. al Coda

all your love ___ and all I gave you was good-bye. _____ So,

CODA

I miss ___ your

tan skin, ___ your sweet smile, ___ so good to me, ___ so

back to De-cem - ber, turn around and change my own mind.

I go back to De-cem - ber all the time,

all the time.

THE BOYS OF FALL

Words and Music by CASEY BEATHARD
and DAVE TURNBULL

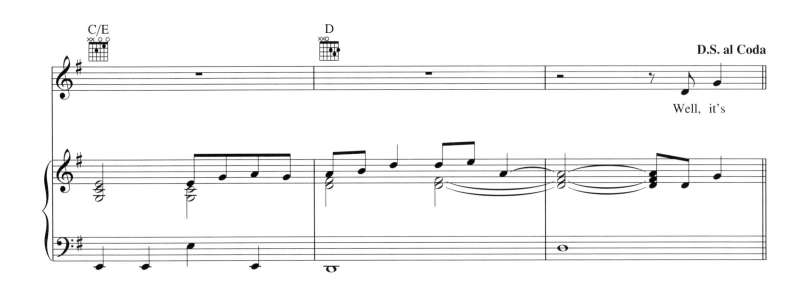

the boys ____ of fall. _____

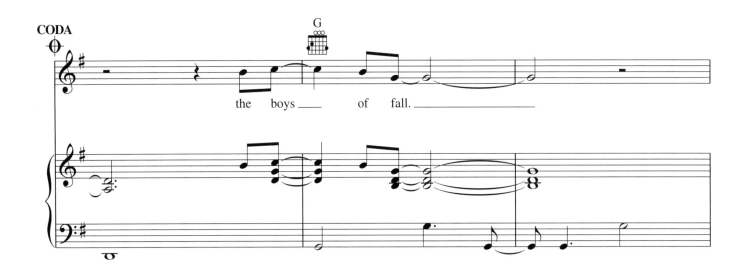

THE BREATH YOU TAKE

Words and Music by CASEY BEATHARD,
DEAN DILLON and JESSIE DILLON

DON'T YOU WANNA STAY

Words and Music by JASON SELLERS,
PAUL JENKINS and ANDY GIBSON

* Recorded a half step higher.

34

THE HOUSE THAT BUILT ME

Words and Music by TOM DOUGLAS
and ALLEN SHAMBLIN

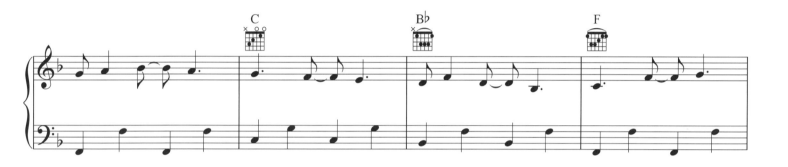

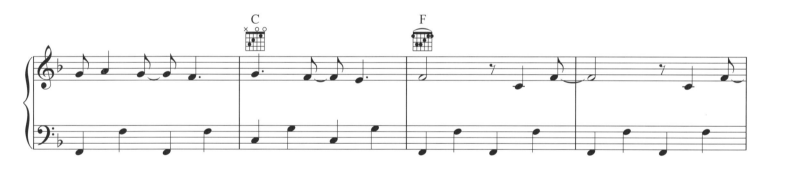

I know they say _____ you

GIMME THAT GIRL

Words and Music by RHETT AKINS,
DALLAS DAVIDSON and BEN HAYSLIP

IN COLOR

Words and Music by JAMEY JOHNSON,
LEE MILLER and JAMES OTTO

seen it in ___ col - or." ___

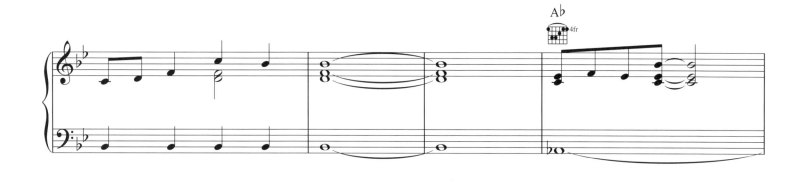

RAIN IS A GOOD THING

Words and Music by DALLAS DAVIDSON
and LUKE BRYAN

My dad-dy spent his life look-in' up at the sky.
Ain't noth-in' like a kiss out back in the barn.

He'd cuss, kick the dust, say-in', "Son, it's way too dry."
Wring-in' out our soak-in' clothes, rid-in' out a thun-der-storm. When the

MAMA'S SONG

Words and Music by LUKE LAIRD,
KARA DioGUARDI, MARTI FREDERIKSEN
and CARRIE UNDERWOOD

THE MAN I WANT TO BE

Words and Music by BRETT JAMES
and TIM NICHOLS

but, Lord, ___ don't ___ give up on ___ me. ___

I wan - na be a giv - in' man. ___ I wan - na real - ly start

OUR KIND OF LOVE

Words and Music by HILLARY SCOTT,
CHARLES KELLEY, DAVE HAYWOOD
and busbee

PUT YOU IN A SONG

Words and Music by KEITH URBAN,
SARAH BUXTON and JEDD HUGHES

Moderately fast

Well, here ___ you come a - gain and you're
sing a - bout your smile and your

look - in' so fine. You don't ___ no - tice me, ___ but it's al - right. I'm just a
pret - ty blue eyes, the way ___ your hair shim - mers in the sun - light. It - 'd

90

TEMPORARY HOME

Words and Music by ZAC MALOY,
LUKE LAIRD and CARRIE UNDERWOOD

Little boy, six years old, a little too used to be-in' a-lone.
Young mom on her own, she needs a little help, got no-where to go.
An-oth-er new mom and dad,
She's look-in' for a job, look-in' for a way

WATER

Words and Music by KELLEY LOVELACE,
BRAD PAISLEY and CHRIS DUBOIS

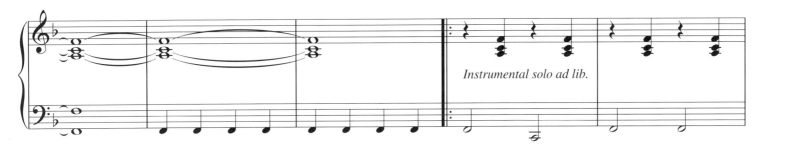

Instrumental solo ad lib.

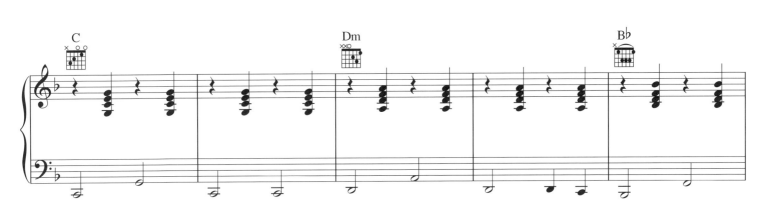

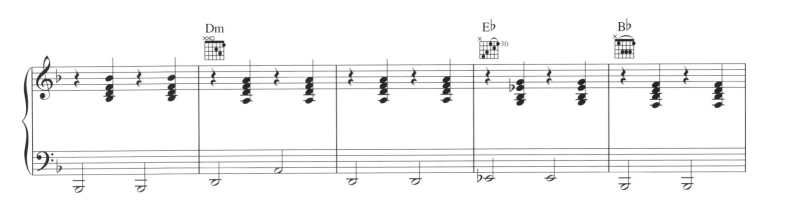

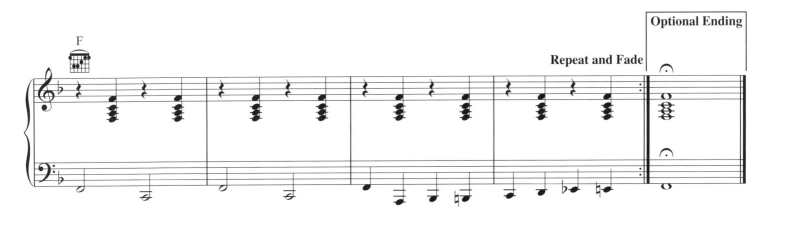

WHY DON'T WE JUST DANCE

Words and Music by JIM BEAVERS,
JONATHAN SINGLETON and DARRELL BROWN

WHY WAIT

Words and Music by TOM SHAPIRO,
NEIL THRASHER and JAMES YEARY

STUCK LIKE GLUE

Words and Music by SHY CARTER,
KRISTIAN BUSH, JENNIFER NETTLES
and KEVIN GRIFFIN

Moderately fast

Ab - so - lute - ly no one that knows me _____ bet - ter,

no _____ one that can make me feel so _____ good.

How __ did we stay so long to - geth - er _____ when ev -

* Recorded a half step lower.